T0370509

ALONG THESE ROADS WE TRAVEL

Poems

JOANN RITA VEGA

iUniverse books may be ordered through booksellers or by contacting:

iUniverse
1663 Liberty Drive
Bloomington, IN 47403
www.iuniverse.com
844-349-9409

ISBN: 978-1-6632-0905-4 (sc)
ISBN: 978-1-6632-0914-6 (e)

Library of Congress Control Number: 2020917611

Print information available on the last page.

iUniverse rev. date: 09/07/2021

CONTENTS

DEDICATION

For the light in all of us. For my guru. For my teacher at the foothills of the Himalayas. For my daughter and granddaughter, Ingrid and Lia. For John.

To my mother and father, whose memory guides me.

INTRODUCTION

In these poems by Joann Rita Vega, several elements blend neatly together: light and shadow; men and women; thought and action; and above all, as the very form suggests, a multicultural examination. The words are those of one who has witnessed the silent anguish of others.

The themes are many, but Ms. Vega's concern with love and war; happiness and unhappiness; transcendence of human ego; as well as a natural acceptance and welcoming of all cultures make these poems.

Not unnaturally, one wishes to empathize with the unfailing and unflagging optimism that prevails in these poems. Yet, this work is not a plea for a better world or a mere denunciation of our own. The important significance which gives life to any poem is not what it says—our politicians and priests do that for us—but how it is said. Here is the true success with this volume of verses: Ms. Vega has differing tones and a specific voice that addresses with directness each differing experience.

A great deal of rhythm is in the build-up of lines, in the accumulated meaning of words, as they move through the poem. Probably the poems that succeed the best are those on which there is no public outcry but a still, small, sensible voice not decrying, not denouncing, but merely articulating a situation with which we may all empathize. The fact that the reader is almost conscripted into a changed alliance, a new assortment of values, is at the core of the poetry.

This book is not only about her words. It is also about the author's other form of focusing the situations she immerses herself into—her photography. It is said a picture is worth a thousand words. It is in this light Joann Rita Vega uses her photography to complement her work.

Joann Rita Vega

Some of the poems have been published in journals and magazines, but many are here for the first time. Altogether they represent the development of a woman of sensibilithy as she attempts to wrestle with the times in which we live and to chart some alternatives for herself and others. She does not ask us to agree, only to listen.

Raymond P. Del Papa
Poet, historical writer, social justice activist, award-winning railroad photographer

TO A LOST POEM

All these silent syllables
Came to me and left.
They left,
Floating in the warm afternoon,
Alive and free.

If I would have written them today,
They would have died in my pen.

Oh, Poetry, eternal,
You belong to the Infinite!

TO THE PUERTO RICAN MAN
WHO READ MY BOOK

In a warm October morning.
We, you and I, sat in your white painted office.
And you seemed very serious that morning,
As you accused me of two terrible deeds:
Traveling to my homeland too often.
Writing a poetry book, you said you had completely read.

The color of your walls, I noticed.
Not a painting, not a photograph.

Not an indication of the human soul, and
Because of that, I doubted you had really read my words.

My book. My poor, simple book.
I asked with great innocence, "Where did you find it?"
And from the white painted walls,
Your eyes looked down with indifference.

You said you read my book. Did you pay for the cost?

Then you said I travelled to Cuba too often in a year.
Do you travel to Puerto Rico often?
Do you visit your parents?
Your uncles and aunts?
Your cousins and your old neighborhoods?

Do you travel to your beautiful land?
Your eyes animated with a certain humane light.

"Yes, I travel, just like you," said I.
For, like you, I love my uncles and aunts.
And my cousins. And my old neighborhoods.

You and I, two Caribbean neighbors,
Meeting by historical hazards in this white painted room.

Not your office. Neither mine.

REVELACIÓN

La arena gira en círculos de caracoles y
Un puño de olas brillantes
Se levanta desde el mar,
Formando un arcoíris
Bajo el cielo que ruge su tormenta.

El látigo cae y se agita con premura diabólica
Sobre los cuerpos mutilados.
Los vencidos cuerpos,
Que nunca olvidaron y que se levantan,
Con alaridos fieros,
Empujados por renovados torrentes de sangre.

Oro.
Cadenas.
Desamparo.
Racismo.
Inversiones.
Hambre.

La tierra tiembla.
Se estremece el continente pisoteado.
El continente
llagado de plantaciones y de destrucción climática.

El mar levanta sus olas
Con amenaza apocalíptica.
La naturaleza gime.
Su nombre es América,
Bajo la bota de la civilización.

Se agita el universo !
Colón despierta de su sueño.
Se sacude los pies en la arena ensangrentada.

THE CALYPSONIAN

Jonas arrived at the beach today,
As always, early,
With his wife and his big-eyed daughter,
With skin lighter than his.

When the sun came up,
Already his wife was preparing
The fritter stand
On the shore.

Very cheap shark fritters
For tourists to buy,

Sitting at the rustic tables
Under the coconut trees.

Jonas's small guitar
Is ready for the improvised calypso.

Today, and like every day,
His music will not speak of him
Nor of his dreams.
Neither of his struggle for a better life.

Today, he will sing to the tourist,
Who will find it all interesting and beautiful,
Even Jonas's hungry face.

Some coins
They throw him in the old hat
While Jonas looks at them, smiles, sings, and hates.

When the sun disappears
Behind the deep green mountains,
Three tired figures
Walk away along the beach.

Jonas, with his guitar under his arm,
Counts the profits of an entire day
Of hiding himself behind his smile.

"Damn it!"
He finally says, already in his loneliness,
And his face is pursed
While the three vanish under the trees.

WAR

The war continues,
But now you are gone.
Dream.
Enemies we were.
One.
In this unfolding never-ending struggle.

The essential, same.
Divided, yes, and yet united.
One.

Enemies yet brothers.
One.
The game, eternal.
Dream.

Only the pieces move, and
One day, disappear.
Dream.
Eternal.
One.

YOUR EYES

In your eyes,
My ancestors meet.
In your eyes,
I can see the ocean softly bathing the shores,
Of loved ancestral islands,
Dreaming of a forgotten past
That has never reached the consciousness.

In your eyes,
In your noble and transcending eyes,
I can feel my past, advancing toward me, as in a dream,
Struggling to become known and lively.

Your eyes
Speak of love.
Your eyes
Speak of strength.
Your eyes
Speak of struggle,
And force,
Of pain and deceit,
Of betrayal and forgiveness,
Of poverty and transcendence,
Of exploitation and resilience.

Your eyes
Stand before me like an invitation.
Your eyes
Are bringing hope into my soul.

ABRIL DE 1984

Todo está en calma ahora.
Y el viento cruza a grandes pasos
Las calles humeantes.

Entre lamentos de miedo
Santo Domingo yace, cansada y llorosa,
Después de la pelea.

Fueron unos pocos, los hombres primero.
Las mujeres y los niños vinieron luego.
A la hora de la tarde,
Ya eran quinientos los hambrientos.

Todo está en calma ahora,
Y el aire que viene del mar
Limpia el olor de la sangre.

Nada se escucha, nada,
Sólo el golpear de las olas y
El gemido de alguien llorando a su muerto.

Un día más ha terminado.
Mañana será otro igual,
De hambre y esperanzas.
Luego, muchos más, los suficientes,
Para que todos olviden que en este día, ya viejo,
Murieron sus hermanos por hambre.

RETURN

Daylight.
Outside myself is the pain
I contemplate.
Outside myself is the desire
I do not feel.

Far from vain ideals is my being
And the love that unites me
To other creatures of this world.

Beyond the vast horizons
Is the home that awaits me
In the deepest level of my being.

I am Light.
I leave on an unending voyage toward my center,
Traveling through an impenetrable, agitated, yet calm ocean,
That takes me once and once again
Toward the shore.

I have given all, and yet,
All have remained stronger
But different.

I now discard all my old possessions
And the new acquisitions of my mind.
I travel through this eternal night
Toward daylight.

WOMAN IN THE CITY

Island woman
Passing by,
Passing me by.

"Hello,"
She greets me.
"How are tings?"

"They are fine."
"And you."
"How are you?"

Smiling woman,
Happy-looking woman
Passing by.

"Oh, I am well,"
(smile)
"Except,
I asphyxiate on the asphalt,
And I miss my home,
And the growing trees by the river,
And I wish I didn't have to greet people
In a different language.
So distant.
So foreign.
But, oh!
I am fine.
I even smile."

Smiling woman,
Passing by,
Hurrying woman,
Busy-looking woman,
Sad,
Lost-in-the-distance woman,
Passing me by.

A STORY FROM MY PEOPLE

I remember Nicolas when I was a child,
And my eyes were glad to see him pass every day,
Dragging his worn old shoes
Down the long street toward his little house on the side of the road
Near the river that crossed the city.
His face was kind and worried when he quietly
Walked, not noticing the presence of others.

Nicolas.
The old Black man everyone thought crazy
Spent his days with his old machete in his hand, looking for Spaniards
Because, according to his memories, he had been a Mambi.

With every night and day he lived on this earth,
His soul became more passionately united to the Dead of his Nganga,
His only true possession for many years buried in the back of his house.
To his Dead, he made daily oblations.
To his Dead, he gave his Soul, and they became One.

The townspeople told me
That on an unforgettably sad morning,
His family tied him to a tree on the estate,
Because there was not a doubt that poor Nicolas was crazy.

They also told me that, on the first night,
When his wife Michaela went to take him food,
She could not find Nicolas tied to the tree.
And that when she desperately ran home,
A blue butterfly fluttered over her,
And the echo of a deep and painful ancestral cry
Coming from the depths of the ether
Made her faint on the narrow road.

Days passed.
Then months passed.
And the blue butterfly fluttered under the sun all day long.
And when the children in the neighborhood tried to catch her,
It disappeared.

The neighbors told me
That on the dark and quiet nights of summer,
When the crossing of the river waters was gently heard,
The butterfly snoozed over the Nganga in the yard of the house.
It flew around the land for months … many months.
And on a bright, sunny day, it softly disappeared.

Joann Rita Vega

And the neighbors also tell me
That a faint flutter of wings is still heard on the field
Through all these long years,
On the quiet summer nights.

THE BELL

To the memory of Andrei Tarkovsky.

Here we stand, my brother,
Amidst this flawless,
Always unfolding universe.

In the center of our hearts
Lies inscrutable knowledge
We will never learn, for no one may teach it.

Joann Rita Vega

Eternal and yet ephemeral is our presence, a bliss,
Living in the passion of an always present, evolving miracle.
No Sin, for there is a reason in every step we take.

In the center of our hearts,
In the center of what has lived, and in the center of all that will ever live
Vibrates a Song.
The Eternal Toll of a Bell,
Forgotten
But present in every measure of its vibration,
Encompassing humanity's dream,
Asserting we are infinite and that all knowledge is eternal.

Nothing to learn, my brothers … nothing to learn.
For we have always known and preserved it all
From the beginning.

SERENIDAD

Cuando recuerdo,
Tratando de vislumbrar más allá de estas aguas,
Que cargan secretos demasiado intrincados
Para mi entendimiento humano.
Memorias, sueños de caminatas pasadas,
Recogiendo caracoles en la orilla
De la mano de mi padre,
Se reúnen y vienen a golpear mi corazón
Con fuerza creciente,
Que vibra a través
De mis días, pasados y presentes.

Joann Rita Vega

Mi mente descansa, imperturbable,
Quieta, soberbia, solemne.
No pensamiento, no razón, no esperanza.
Solamente un sueño que se rompe,
Por lo que hoy soy.

Y, me pregunto desde la profundidad de mis recuerdos:
Por qué soy aún sensible a esta idea,
A pesar de de todos estos largos años,
Como en el primer día en que dejé la orilla ?

Mi corazón llora.
Mi alma está perdida.
Mi cuerpo está marcado con el dolor
Que nos pertenece a todos.

Aislada, como si no entendiera,
Mi mente descansa, imperturbable, tranquila,
En serenidad egocéntrica,
Lejos de mi corazón,
Que ahora me entiende.

A STRANGE TRAVELER I AM

What a strange traveler I am.
I make plans at night by my bedside light,
And I discuss them with my pillow
And make all pertinent preparations and schedules to follow.

I have suddenly decided, this morning,
Not to go up to the mountains
And visit Simla.

This morning, I have decided to stay by the River
And speak all day to my Mother Ganges.
Another day I will go to the mountains.

Joann Rita Vega

Today, I will sit here, by the River and speak to Mother.
So many stories I have to tell her.
So many songs I have to sing her.

I have to tell her how much I have missed her presence
And how delighted I am to touch her waters today
And rejoice myself in her magnificent quiet dance as she looks into my eyes
With unfathomable love, bringing my ancient tears upon her transparent lap.

Another day, I will go to Simla,
But not today.
Not today.

WALKING BY THE GANGES

To Rishikesh and the Old Renunciant

No farewells in the summer of last year.
After my last morning walking along the Ganges,
I did not see you again
Sitting on the bench by the river, trying to navigate the deepest routes
Of your inner world.

The sun is dancing its usual morning dance from behind
Sleepy mountains, and they color the waters
With glistening greyish-green tones,
Like my inner promise to return.

Joann Rita Vega

I have returned.
And this morning, I have again saluted my Mother,
The Mother of all.
And the sun has already displayed its flirting dances
From behind the mountains.

And I look for you,
Along the path of the River,
And the vessel of your bench is empty.
No one is trying to navigate the deepest routes of his inner worlds today.

And I think. And I fear little human fears.
Maybe you have lost yourself within the mighty waters.
Maybe the sun has taken you into its kingdom
And I won't be able to see you again.
Maybe.
Maybe.

But, this early morning,
Down the revered road, I see
Three happy figures, chatting and laughing with earthly laughter,
Advance toward me.
Om. Tat. Sat!

My friend is laughing!
My friend is walking his eternal walk by the Ganges!
Oh, my Lord Shiva, what an enchantment!

VIAJE A LA TIERRA LEJANA

Mi madre habló en la gran cocina,
En donde los antepasados se reunían en un tiempo
Alrededor de suculentos platos,
En días de grandes celebraciones.
Las paredes grises, cargadas de los años y la ausencia,
Le devolvieron, una a una, sus palabras.

- Hoy prepararemos cuatro mesas largas.
- Tres para los mayores.
- Una para los muchachos.
(Yo era uno de ellos entonces),
Habló la voz de mi abuela desde su estertor solitario.

-Que prepararemos hoy? Dijo mi madre,
desde su locura sin recuerdos.
- Hoy es un gran día.
- Ayer se vendió toda la cosecha.
- Yo me voy temprano a ver el sol !

Me alimento hoy de esta gran casa,
Por donde corría cuando niña
En los días bulliciosos de verano.

Hoy es un gran día !
Hoy vendrán Todos !
Los vivos y los muertos !

Tío Pepe se sentará, como siempre, a la cabeza de la mesa
y dejará su sudario colgado detrás de una puerta.
Tia Niña, le servirá el arroz y la carne con cariño.
No se han visto en tanto tiempo !
Abuela, envuelta en su voluminoso cuerpo irá y vendrá preocupada,
Bañada por la luz del recuerdo de sus nietos.

Todos nos reuniremos en esta tarde de mayo,
Y como siempre, cada cual ha de contar su historia.
Y entre risas y recuerdos, nos alegraremos sobre este viejo y mudo patio.
Sobre este largo, amante patio, que callado nos espera,
A pesar de las distancias y del tiempo.

Mi padre, ha de llegar con paso lento, preocupado como siempre,
Y se ha de sentar, sin un sitio preferido,
A un costado de la mesa.

Cuantos recuerdos !
Cuanto cansancio en su mirada sin comienzo !
Ante la mirada suplicante de mi abuela.

Cuanta lejanía sin razón !
Silencio !
Lágrimas que no cayeron antes.
Silencio !
Y ha quedado, sin presente. Sin pasado,
Como en su primera y última cena.
Silencio !

La cocina se ha llenado, lentamente,
De un suave olor fraternal,
Que sólo conoció en otros tiempos.

Los calderos cantan y se alegran.
Y el olor de especies se extiende por el universo.
Silencio !

Hoy, hay una gran luz en esta gran casa.
En la casa de mi abuela.
En la casa de mis sueños.
Una gran luz.
Gran luz eterna !
Una gran Luz de Todos !
Que viajará conmigo,
Mañana, al salir el alba.

TIMELESS

To my father.

I shall never behold again this fancy,
For it is now leaving me.
The spark of your pupil will return once again to the flames,
And it is there where I must find you from this moment.

Let's you and I, oh ancient wine,
Bow to the star on the horizon
Until night will become, finally, morning.

The silence of the void is with me now,
And this silence is the stone
That will support my soul.

In the silky softness of my breath,
Between the dreams and the conscience,
Will your contour return to validate my memories?
Will this Love become love again?

Only this rock of silence
Has the answer to this secret.

Nothing is left to be pronounced nor thought.
Only the beats of my heart,
Trying to stop this dream from fading,
Are left amidst the times.

Joann Rita Vega

UNIVERSAL THUNDER

Crying of fear.
There comes the wind.
Crying of anguish.
There come the tears,
And the desperation
For not being able to change the order.

Crying rain.
Crying tears.
Crying for the thunder,
Stronger on the mountains.

Crying desperation.
So many dreams.
What beautiful earth.
What agony!

Ah … He hides among the trees.
He runs.
He falls.
Ah … He falls,
the hero of the poor,
the dreamer,
has succumbed.

The rain is descending over the tired earth.
The tears are arriving,
The tears of the poor.
Only they know.

Thunders of war.
And the man runs.
Only he knows.

He kisses God.
He kisses the poor.
He sings a song to the roses.

Ah … He smiles. That beautiful smile.
Ah … He sings. The beautiful song of mankind.
What Chorus of Children.

Joann Rita Vega

What a Lighted Candle
Looks after his dreams.

What woman hopes in the distance,
Trembling of fear?
There comes the wind.
Crying in anguish.

And the desperation
For not being able to change the order.
Crying rain.
Crying tears.
Crying thunder.
Crying mountains.

TI GASON

Ti gason !
Ki kote out eye ?
Te he buscado toda la mañana !

Mwen te nan rivye a madam.

Por qué estabas en el río, ti gason ?

Oh, mwen tale pou we si liberte te bo rivye a.

Has visto a la libertad por el río, ti gason ?

Joann Rita Vega

Wi Madam, mwen te we li !
Li te mete you rob blan,
Kankou you pigon, epi van an !
Ella reía, reía.
Ella cantaba, cantaba.
Y los pájaros del río, cantaban con ella !

Mwen te we li, Madam !
Mwen te we li !
Era muy hermosa !
Con el sol en los ojos !

Eske li te paleak ou ti gason?
Sí. Ella me habló.
Epi li di mwen.
Vini we mwen!
Et puis li bo mwen.

Yo no soy de aquí.
Dile a los otros, si quieren encontrarme,
Deben subir a la montaña.

Allí, soy reina.
Mwen glorifie sang pep la.
Allí canto otras canciones.
Mwen chante kourage, batay, et sacrifice.
Si alguien cae,
Yo le cubro el rostro de Sol.

Ale la vil la, ti gason !
Corre por las calles de Arcaie.
Port au Prince, y Port au Pe!

Ale tout kote sou la te
Et di yo
Di yo tout, ti gason !
Ke mwen a prale la.
Vengan a buscarme !

Oh, vini ti pitit!
Vini pou mwen ka bo ou !
Oh, ti gason.
Ahora, ya eres un hombre !

Joann Rita Vega

SHIVA!

Your Name, I salute!
I salute You today.
Father.
Without and with Form. Smeared with the Ashes of
Succumbed worlds and civilizations.

Creator. Sustainer. Dissolver of Worlds.
Minds, Bodies, Souls
Are made from You.
Oh, Sequence from the Subtlest to the Grossest.
Oh, Unforgettable Presence.
Unforgettable Teacher of Universal Truth.
Memories I carry within the games of Your world,
Its dreams and awakenings, in unending circles.

Shiva!
Your energy defines and liberates us.
Your Power gives us a clear concept of our worlds.
Teacher of Truth! Protector of the Real.
Destroyer of our Evil and Illusions of Grandeur.
Protector of the Poor.
The One who speaks through their eyes.
Embodiment of compassion.
I Salute You today!

Photographs from every angle of this living dream of yours
My mind carries under Your Power.
The beggar, the dispossessed. The one who believes to have All.
The monastery, the battlefield, the church,
The tombstone, where a dream lies forever.
The last ritual toward the Eternal Fire,
Toward your next world.

Shiva.
Patron of Yogis,
Creator and Protector of the Vedas,
Absolute Owner of our Highest Consciousness,
Ganges waters flowing through your hair.

Entire Creation
Present in all opposing ideals.
Oh, Universal Soul of Consciousness,
Lead us to salvation in these difficult times.

This photographer, from her dream, takes her dreaming images
Once more and offers them to You.
Shiva. My Teacher.
You, I salute
And beg for Mercy.

THE LONGEST NIGHT

Silence, please, do not disturb.
My child sleeps in the barracks in a distant land.

Silence, please.

This night is unending and tormenting,
And all the prayers of my aching soul come to visit
In this long night, the longest night of my life.

And in this dark time of my soul, I claim, I reach,
I speak now with Allah.

Joann Rita Vega

Silence, please.

I ignore the wind outside my window.
I ignore the voice of some lost soul,
Asking for forgiveness on its way to the infinite.

Allah, My All.
Allah, my only sweet companion.
You bring me peace in this night of horrible nightmares and pleas.

My God of the Universe.
In every name I call you mine.
My Allah. My God. My Brahman. My Nameless One.

I now thank You from this Soul that is You.
I thank You now from this Heart that guards your Agni.

Silence, please. Do not disturb!
My child and I sleep in the Valley of Allah tonight.

STREET MAN

One, two, three, four, five, six,
Seven ... seventy-seven spoons of soil.
One, two, three, four, five, six, seven ...
Seventy-seven breaths from the soul,
In the midst of this noisy street.

One Spirit.

A man bringing a message,
One, two, three, four, five, six, seven …
Seventy-seven spoons of soil.
Seventy-seven breaths from the soul.
His eyes are dark with wisdom—or madness, perhaps.

One Spirit.

His language full of fancy,
Among the others' worldly intonations,
Two, three, four, five, six, seven …
Seventy-seven spoons of soil.
Seventy-seven breaths from the soul.
A perfect equation, he enounces
While adjusting his belt over the raggedy pants
Under the blue skies.

One Spirit.

One, two, three, four, five, six, seven …
Seventy-seven spoons of soil
Taken daily.
He speaks his truth.
Seventy-seven breaths from the soul.

One Spirit.

He speaks to everyone, the man,
And some listen with attention
While others smile and contemptuously leave.
He knows, dares to say.

One Spirit.

One, two, three, four, five, six, seven …
Seventy-seven breaths from the soul.
The man walks away, distracted, repeating his truth
And becomes lost in the busy street.

One Spirit.

A TRANSCENDING MORNING BY TOE RIVER

All is quiet,
And a veil of silence surrounds morning like a hand
Trying to grasp an escaping dream.
Not a word. Not a breath is heard,
Only the mellow rhythm of a Heart singing.
Silently singing.

Only the embracing words of an unconscious god
Are heard in this magnificent morning.
And the sound of this gently flowing river
Bathing one by one, like a caring father, the unearthed rocks,

Brings me to realize the image of another River,
Dancing. Always dancing,
Majestically rolling. Electric. Ethereal.
Sparkling with the colors of infinite's eternal energies.

Silence and the soft cool morning air
And the greenish dressing of the trees,
Swaying their leaves in a mystical, enchanting chorus
Over the illusive grayish colors of decay.

Silence, beyond the joyfully singing of wrens, cardinals, and hummingbirds,
Claiming full ownership of this morning.
Eternal presence, softly mingling amidst this most sacred beauty.
Morning's silence, in which I can hear the eternal voice
Of all encompassing harmony.

THE CITY SLEEPS

And Papa Hogoun whispers an ancestral mixture of metallic sounds.
There, over the high mountains
That tear the clouds with their green knives.

Silence. Great Silence.
Mystery. Great Mystery.

Falling
Over the old, great conquered city.

No one knows.

But the city bleeds.
The city
That never again saw the light
Since the day
In which Columbus suffered on its shore
His fever of discovery
And then covered it with shadows.

City of Black laughter.
City of Black tears.
Dreams of the military.
Dreams of investors.
French.
North Americans.
English.

Small hopes
Among the repeated failures.
Blood
That runs down the streets.
Their streets.
Our streets.

Papa Hogoun wanders
Through the foggy afternoon,
Engrossed in his own thoughts.
In silence. Thinking.
Planning.

Joann Rita Vega

SHE WAS BY THE RIVER

In the morning, as I walked toward the shy sunlight, I saw her.
She was sobbing, sitting on the bank of Ganges.
The agonies of love. She was sobbing.

And her soft back bones trembled with her every breath.
I saw her as I passed by,
And I felt compassion.

In the evening, on my way to the Prayer Ghat,
I saw her again. She was still sitting on the riverbank.
I saw her again, but she was not sobbing.

And she was still sitting there, like in an ecstatic vision.
As if offering herself to the undulant, glimmering waters
Under her feet.

She was there, melting herself with her own peaceful silence.
Melting with the Joy of Love.
The River, quietly observing, like the Atman.
An ancient image.

I fell on my knees
And, in my own silence,
I uttered a prayer.

PRISIONERA

Gracias por aquel vestido negro.

Tan sólo ayer, yo bien recuerdo tu mirada y tu tristeza,
Me dijiste que tenías miedo, mientras nos abrazamos.
Y hoy ya no estás aquí,
En este espacio habitual en donde conversábamos.

Te han llevado lejos, al presidio.

La sociedad en su ceguera, no imagina siquiera
Que el presidio ya lo llevas dentro.

En tu alma. En tus ojos.
Desde el día en que naciste.

Conocíste tu falta de libertad, el día
En que por primera vez, miraste a la sombría calle,
Por donde cruzaban en apuro,
Los sueños de tus antepasados,
Anteponiendose a los tuyos.

Los sueños de todos.

También sabías,
Que las cárceles del alma y de la voluntad son más oscuras, y
Que hieren, mucho más, las esposas del desprecio.

Sentías miedo ayer.
Miedo terrible de perder la poca libertad
Que una vez tuviste.

Tan sólo ayer, amiga, me dijiste
Que te llevaban al presidio.

Pero yo ya lo sabía, por las lágrimas en tus ojos.
Lo sabía muy bien,
Porque yo también, debo confesar.
Siento miedo.

PREFIERO

Prefiero soñar
Un sueño de amor.
Porque es todo lo que ahora importa.

Prefiero soñar
Un sueño de flores.
De niños jugando.

Prefiero soñar
Un sueño de paz.
De maestros enseñando.

Prefiero soñar un sueño de palomas.
De cielos azules.
De praderas cubiertas de verde,
No de cenizas.

Prefiero soñar,
Un sueño de mil estrellas.
Un sueño de toda la humanidad.

Trabajando.
Amando.
Marchando.
Unidos.

POR ESTA CALLE

Esta calle de recuerdos en donde yo nací,
Está rodeada de pequeñas casas,
Que hoy veo vestidas con
Los viejos y amables colores de antaño.

Los largos portales se estrechan,
Unidos en fuerte y filial abrazo.
Parece que se aman, como los hombres
Que diariamente viven y mueren en las casas.

Así veo mi calle, así
La siento, brillante como las estrellas
Del cielo cubano que la cubre.

Llena de juegos pasados sobre
Sus desnudas piedras.

Aquí, en ésta minúscula, en ésta
Honorable y perdida calle,
Viven los amigos de mi padre
Que, como robles,
Cargan con orgullo sus años.

Están todos aquí.
No falta nadie,
En esta mesa diaria.

Todos van y vienen,
llenos de luz.
Como niños.
Como soles eternos.

En esta calle noble y larga
en donde yo nací.
En esta calle estrecha
En donde pasé mi juventud.
En esta honorable calle …
Viven todos los hombres del mundo.

OF MARBLE WAS MY DREAM

How did the journey end?
Did he cry at the time of his departure
Like the old marble statue he showed me in my dream?
He smiled at me when he saw my tears,
And his eyes were the eyes of God.

Death. Death. You have no glory.
The body disappears, but the joys of love
Forever remain.

The music of life is present,
But forgetfulness kills the love
And the beloved.
Did he cry at the time of his departure?
And his eyes were still the eyes of God?
I was not there. At this most sacred moment.
But my heart deeply wishes so.

Death takes the body,
But the joy of Life forever remains.
The music of Life is ever present.
Like the Beloved.

Joann Rita Vega

NICOLÁS

Recuerdo a Nicolás, desde cuando era una niña.
Y mis ojos se alegraban al verlo cruzar,
Arrastrando sus gastados y viejos zapatos,
Por la larga calle, hacia su pequeña casa a un costado del camino,
Cerca del río, que cruzaba la ciudad.
Su rostro era amable y dulce, cuando caminaba
Callado, sin notar la presencia de los otros.

Nicolás.
El hombre viejo y negro que todos creian loco,
Pasaba sus días con el viejo machete en la mano,
Buscando españoles
Porque en sus recuerdos, había sido un Mambí.

A cada noche, su alma se unía, apasionadamente,
Al Muerto de su Nganga,
Que había enterrado, hacía ya muchos años, en el patio de su casa.

Me contaron sus vecinos,
Que en una triste mañana,
Su familia lo encerró en un cuarto fuera de la casa,
Porque ya no habia dudas de que estaba loco.

Me contaron que en la primera noche
En que su esposa Micaela fué a llevarle comida,
Ya no lo encontró,
Y que asustada corrió a su casa,
Mientras una mariposa azul revoloteaba sobre ella
Y el eco de un profundo llanto,
Viniendo desde la profundidad del éter,
La hizo desmayar sobre el estrecho camino.

Pasaron los días.
Luego, pasaron los meses,
Y la mariposa azul revoloteaba bajo el sol durante todo el día.
Y cuando los muchachos del barrio intentaban atraparla,
Desaparecía.

También me contaron los vecinos,
Que en las noches oscuras y tranquilas de verano,
Cuando el correr de las aguas del río se escuchaba suavemente,
La mariposa dormitaba sobre la Nganga, en el patio de la casa.

Pasaron largos meses.
Y en un día de sol brillante, ya no volvieron a verla.

Y me cuentan también los vecinos,
Que un revoloteo tenue aún se escucha por el campo,
A través de todos estos largos años,
En las noches calladas de verano.

NAMASTE

As we meet in the mornings.
Namaste.
As we all walk by the Ganges.
Namaste.

Namaste in the evenings
As we gather for our prayers.
Smiles on people.
Friendly faces.
Namaste.

I bow to the friendly offering of milk
And to the offering of water
And to the cooked fish,
Served by my beloved friends.

I bow to the land and her gifts
And to the people and their hopes.
I deeply bow to the knowledge of the Sages
And the height and grandeur of Vedanta
And the deeply seated love for a Higher Self.

I bow to All
As I bow to myself.
Namaste.
Namaste.
Namaste.
Om.

LOTUS

Como estatua de mármol
Estabas frente a mí, ante la inmensidad de las aguas.
Trayendo la figura final de tu verdadera existencia.
Incontables diseños de tu pasado y tu presente.

Así descansas, sin cuidado alguno ante tu reino.
Tranquilo. Egocéntrico.
Dominando el entorno en el que por siempre has vivido.
Yo desde aquí, te contemplo.
Y desde mi más profunda identidad te admiro y además, te amo.

Esta vez, he regresado.
Y de nuevo he corrido a saludarte, luego de un año de nostalgias, viejo amigo.
He venido rápido, corriendo a traves del tiempo y la distancia,
Evitando a las gentes apuradas.
Y aquí te encuentro. Como en un milagro.
Como en un milagro.

Aquí te dejé. Oh magnífico dios de viejos tiempos.
Y hoy aquí te encuentro.

Mi corazón renace. Hoy, de nuevo creo en el milagro de la vida.
Aquí estás, frente a mi descansando, impasible como siempre.
Separado de las voces y la multitudes. Dios único y perfecto.

Te amo tanto, Lotus.
Como el primer dia en que nos vimos, hace ya tanto tiempo.

Ven, comamos juntos de estos dulces.
Comparte conmigo, como siempre, la pobreza de mis caramelos.
Permíteme hoy tocar tu cabellera milenaria,
Pues yo no se que ha de suceder mañana.

Todo ha de cambiar. Asi lo siento.
Y quizás no vuelva por un año, o por algún tiempo.
Mi dios de mármol, egocéntrico y calmado.
Reflección de las fuerzas que alimentan nuestras realidades.

A pesar de todos estos cambios.
A pesar de este dolor humano tan profundo.
Yo regresaré a la orilla de este, nuestro Rio Madre.
Y tu estarás ahí sentado, como siempre. En tu sitio.
Observando. Libre.

MR. BIG MAN, LISTEN TO US!

We are the Soca people.
We are the Merengue people.
We are the Salsa people.

We have been dancing.
We have been laughing.
We have been hungry.
We have been landless
For too long of a time.

What are you going
To do about us,
Mister Big Man?

We have been sad for many years
In spite of our dance,
And the music that we play
On the shore or in the city
Is not enough.

We are the Soca people.
We are the Reggae people.
We are the Salsa people.

We are the dignified people.
We are the surrendered people.
We are the lied-to people.

We are the people who want to sing
But not for you.
For ourselves.

What are you going to do
About us,
Mr. Big Man ?

MOTHER

To Mother Ganges

Mother never sleeps late.
And I have come from the other side of the city,
Carrying this bouquet of flowers
To offer her as soon as she wakes up.

But today, she seems to sleep until late.

And the sun is not showing its glowing face
From the mountains
For fear of waking her up.

Everybody passes by,
Wondering, *Why is Mother*
Still sleeping at this morning hour?

Some people say they saw her dancing on the skies last night,
Wearing a red beautiful dress
Full of colorful lights,
Sparkling with thunderous sounds
As endless rivers of water
Showered the streets in the late hours.
And that is why she still sleeps in her long dream of creation.

Mother lies in the stillness of her waters,
Wrapped in the sheets
of these green morning colors.

All is very quiet … very quiet now.
And the people murmur.
Mother has not awaken yet today.
She sleeps until late this morning.

MY LOTUS

As a statue of the toughest marble,
You seat in front of the vast waters,
Bringing reflections of light from the deepest worlds,
Countless designs of your present and your past.

Thus, you rest without care before this your kingdom,
Facing the waters that ensure your daily existence.
Self-centered, a god.
Master of your surroundings.
I look at you from here,
And from my deepest being, I admire and love you.

I have returned to my India and to you
After a year of nostalgia, my old dear dog.
My heart is reborn. Again, I believe in the miracle of life.
Here you are, in front of me. Resting impassively, as always,
Separated from the voices and the crowds.

Come, please, let us eat these cookies together.
Share with me the poverty of my candies.
Let me touch your ancient hair,
For I don't know what will happen after.
My marble god, self-centered and calm.

In spite of this bitter human pain,
I will always return to this abode. Our shore.
And you will be sitting here as usual. In your place.
Observing. Free. I pray.

LLUVIA SOBRE PORT-AU-PRINCE

La noche ha llegado, despacio,
Envolviéndolo todo en sus sombras.
Y la lluvia cae, fría y ajena, sobre el aeropuerto.
El chic aeropuerto. El artístico aeropuerto.

Esta lluvia nocturna, no molesta aquí a nadie.
Y la gente con sombrero y con blue jeans,
Pasa apurada, hablando lenguas extranjeras.
Desconocidas lenguas de hombres blancos.

En este lugar en donde hoy me encuentro,
No hay hambre, ni frío, ni picadas de viruela.
Todo aquí es hermoso y el aire huele a colonia y a rosas.

Pero, no mires afuera.
No permitas que tus ojos de turista alegre,
Crucen el ilumunado salón y se pierdan en la calle oscura.

No veas turista, que allá en la distancia todo es diferente.
No mires, por favor turista, la fría lluvia,
Que cae mojando a los hombres que andan corriendo
Y hablan creole.

La lluvia que entra, humillante y burlona,
Por los huecos de los techos, mojándolo todo.
Destruyéndolo todo en su caer.

Tampoco allá esta lluvia molesta.
Ya están habituados a este eterno llover,
Año tras año. Siglo tras siglo.

Pero si te empeñas en mirar, turista.
Míralos allá en la distancia,
Callados e inertes. Mirando,
Con ojos cansados de tanto mirar,
El fatídico y constante caer de la lluvia.

Joann Rita Vega

LA CIUDAD DUERME

… Y Papá Ogún susurra
Una mezcla ancestral de sonidos metálicos …
Allá en lo alto de las montañas
Que rasgan las nubes con sus verdes cuchillos.

Silencio. Gran silencio.
Misterio. Gran misterio,
Cayendo, gota tras gota, despacio,
Sobre la vieja, gran,
Conquistada ciudad.

Nadie sabe nada.

La ciudad que se desangra.
La ciudad
Que nunca más vió la luz,
Desde el día
En que Colón padeció sobre sus orillas
Su fiebre de descubrimiento.
Y después, la cubrió de sombras.

Ciudad de risa negra.
Llanto negro.
Ciudad de sueños de militares.
Sueños de inversionistas.
Franceses.
Norteamericanos.
Ingleses.

Llanto negro.

Una pequeña esperanza
Entre los repetidos fracasos.

Sueños de libertad.
Sueños de vida.
Sangre, que corre recta,
Desapareciendo calle abajo.
Tus calles.
Sus calles.
Nuestras calles.

Papa Ogún … deambula
Por el nublado mediodía.
Absorto.
En silencio.

JOSÉ PÉREZ

Nació una mañana de otoño,
Cuando el cielo era gris
Y la esperanza se marchaba con la última brisa.

Sembrador de surcos y de sueños.
Conocedor de profundos secretos
Que la vida le había confiado
Porque era humilde, sencillo y bueno.

Como paloma suave era su sonrisa.
Y su voz, llena de consejos,

Era una caricia diaria en la hora del café mañanero,
Sentado a la pequeña mesa
En donde trazaba el mundo de sus sueños diarios.

Aún recuerdo sus tenues pasos,
Temerosos de despertarme,
Cuando cruzaban por el pasillo largo
Por donde andaban mis ilusiones.

No volví a verlo, luego de aquel año,
En el que conversamos juntos
Bajo la sombra de los árboles del patio.
Su voz fué firme, y a la vez amable.

Quería, que comprendiera que él tenía todo.
Porque vivía de la tierra, que era su amor.
Yo lo comprendí. Lo comprendí muy bien.
Lo comprendió mi alma.
Y mi mano, fué una con la suya.
Y nuestras miradas fueron una visión ancestral.

En una mañana del mes de marzo,
El sol le regaló su último saludo al amanecer.
José abrió su puerta entonces, sonriendo.
Y sus pasos tenues, se perdieron sobre su tierra.
Una suave y breve paloma cruzó hacia el horizonte.

ISLAND

Sitting on the shore of a land so distant,
Gathering, one by one, the intricate pieces
Of my dreams and my hopes.
I well remember.

The veil of the night enshrouds my silence,
And my memory softly travels
To my Motherland,
Which, in silence, has waited for me all these years.

Eternal communion.

And from the depths of this night,
I invoke your name, my dear-distant old friend,
And the names of my ancestors,
To receive my soul upon your shore.

Please, take me, my friend, to see again my island in this dark, inviting night.
Help me to renew my soul with the healing waters of the Land.
Whisper in my ear the songs of the memories and the old hopes of the people.

Take these thoughts, my friend,
That now cross these darkened waters,
And walk with me
In silence.

I will then forget that I once departed.
I will then forget that I am a stranger on a distant land.
Take me. Take me, my old, never-forgotten friend.
Take me with you
To the deepest regions of our land.

I PROPOSE

I simply propose to invite the people,
Everyone,
To join the true celebrations of life.
Here, on our streets, on our yards, in our homes.

On the horizons,
Everywhere, everyone,
On their own mental and spiritual possibilities.

I humbly propose today:
No more separations of humanity.

I propose
That the illiterate join the knowledgeable
And exchange that deepest knowledge
That cannot be learned or taught.

And that they may sing and dance
And enjoy together the daily bread of life,
Without the need to question what the bread is made of
Or who has made it.

The man down the road is dressed in rags,
And he carries Divinity within.
And the man up the road is fancily dressed,
And he carries Divinity within.

I now humbly dare to propose
That all the Gods and Goddesses on the Planet
Undress their divinities at the daily table
And join in the true celebration of Life.

EL VIAJE

Saliste de tu choza temprano, y
Sin saber a donde ibas,
Descalzo, con las viejas ropas raídas,
Seguiste a los que te llevarían a un mundo desconocido,
Detrás de tus verdes montañas.

Y tu mente, sedienta de vida nueva,
Vislumbró otro mundo, en donde encontrarías aire puro.
En donde podrías soñar, hablar y hasta comer.

No te despediste de nadie.
Solamente tus ojos llenos de hambre,
Miraron a las matas de plátano por última vez,
Y a la burra flaca que tantas veces te llevó a la ciudad.

Ella no pudo ir esta vez.
Y tú te fuiste, como un ciego, con tu mujer y tus cinco hijos,
Sin saber a ciertas, a donde te llevaban.

Allá detrás, en la aldea lejana, en un remoto pueblito haitiano,
Quedaron el hambre y las enfermedades,
Que una vez consumieron a tus padres y a casi todos tus amigos.

Por eso, al llegar a la playa reíste alegre.
Y tu risa se oyó frente al mar,
Como se oyen cien caracoles llamando a la guerra.
Pero, no hubo guerra entonces.
Solo tú y tu familia,
Y cincuenta rostros marcados por el hambre y el dolor, subieron al endeble bote,
Que se perdió luego, sobre las verdes aguas del Atlántico,
llevando consigo el secreto de su destino.

Joann Rita Vega

EL EMIGRANTE

El que sería emigrante, a la mañana siguiente
Se levantó temprano y salió a visitar los sitios por donde su alma deambulaba hacía ya muchos
años.

Los techos de la ciudad se desvanecían ante la luz suave del sol, que ya se asomaba.
Anduvo por algún rato, cruzando ante puertas cerradas.
Puertas que él sabía que no volvería nunca a entrar.
Sintió deseos de tocar en alguna, y de esperar que desde algún sueño interrumpido,
Alguien le abriera una nueva aventura.
Pero continuó su camino, sintiéndose poco a poco, un emigrante.

Los emigrantes no miran hacia atrás ni hacia los lados, pensó.
Los emigrantes sólo miran hacia el frente, hacia el futuro que no conocen.
Sólo miran hacia tierras, que no saben como irán a reaccionar bajo sus pasos.

Los emigrantes aprenden, poco a poco, a separarse de amigos íntimos que no volverán a ver.
Porque nunca más volverán a ser íntimos.
Aprenden a pensar en otros nuevos que les esperan en distancias desconocidas.
Comienzan a conocer un mundo con un solo rostro:
El rostro indefinido de los opuestos y de la relatividad.
El rostro de los que realmente fueron.
El rostro de los que nunca serán.
Por eso, no sintió necesidad de visitar a ninguno de sus amigos.

El que sería emigrante,
Se sentó sobre una roca a la salida de la ciudad, y observó:
Trenes que venian de distantes ciudades y que ya no visitaría nunca, ni siquiera en sueños.
Trenes que se alejaban en el horizonte hacia un futuro, más cierto que el de él.
El que seria emigrante, pensó en su niñez.

Pensó en su madre, que desde algún sitio del universo lo esperaba, rodeada de flores, mientras cantaba.

Pensó en su padre, vestido de sus sueños. Destruyendo paredes para encontrarse a sí mismo.

Su padre, perdido en el espiritu de aquella casa, que no lograba comprender.

Su padre, llorando una separación más fuerte que la suya.

Trenes arribando del pasado y del futuro, entrando y saliendo confundidos a la estación.

El que sería emigrante, sacudió la cabeza y se miró a los pies.

Calzaba sus únicos zapatos, compañeros en importantes momentos de su vida.

Sonrió a los recuerdos.

Era todo lo que llevaría en este viaje: zapatos y recuerdos.

La única continuidad presente de su vida.

El que sería emigrante miró a su alrededor.

Todos andaban, demasiado ocupados de sí mismos.

Nadie podría advertir quien faltaría, como él, a la mesa esa noche.

Recordó a la abuela, que ya se convertía en figura lejana. Amada, pero lejana. Perdida en el tiempo.

Por siempre, lejana. Convenciéndole para que no se convirtiera en un emigrante.

Su abuela, que viajaría pronto a través de valles universales. Fuerte como la roca.

Esa roca en donde ahora se sentaba, era su único presente ... y sus zapatos.

Esa roca, le serviría para recostarse eternamente.

Esa roca se convertiría en Yo. En Luz.

El que sería emigrante, guardó la roca en su conciencia.

Silencio. Profundo silencio ... que nunca antes conoció.

El que sería emigrante, supo entonces de un camino nunca andado.

Presente.

La roca cobró fuerza en su conciencia.

Esa roca eterna, sobre la cual la humanidad descansa su identidad perdida.

Lentamente, el que sería emigrante se incorporó. Descalzo, caminó hacia el horizonte.

II

La niebla cubrió el pasado del que sería emigrante.
Ni siquiera recordó el viejo Cristo de su madre, hecho pedazos cuando su fé se terminó.
Ni siquiera recordó su dolor y profundo desprecio ante Aquel que le traicionaba.
Ni el viejo gato que le acompañó por años, y que ahora se escapaba, sin recuerdos,
Sin futuro. Como él, perdido.

El dolor, si es fuerte, hace olvidar sus raíces y su presencia.
Nos convierte en identidad sin dinamo ni estructura.
El dolor todo lo rompe.
Por eso, el que sería emigrante trató de visualizar un futuro, pero no tuvo.
Trató de pertenecer a un pasado, pero no hubo.
Solamente pudo, entonces, aceptar su presente.
Y se recostó sobre la roca que ya era.

Y en aquel momento, el emigrante sintió que nacía.
Sólo. En su propio universo.
Se miró a los pies. No traía sus zapatos. No sabía desde cuando.

Entonces anduvo. El emigrante no supo hacia donde, pero anduvo.
El día había sido largo y pesado. Y la noche se acercaba, confrontando su paso.
El inmigrante se adentró en la noche.

CARIBBEAN PLEA

Monsieur,
Sir,
Señor,

Veinte centavos, por favor.
No tengo que comer.
Mwen pa gen anyen pou'm mange.

Sorry.
I have no money.
Don't bother me.
Leave me alone.

Joann Rita Vega

Míre, estoi enfermo.
Gade, mwen malade.
No tengo que comer.

Don't bother me with your problems.
There is nothing I can do.

Por favor. Por favor, señor.
Tanpri. Tanpri. Msye.

Míra mi cara.
Míra mis huesos.

Your troubles I cannot solve.
Don't bother me now.
Leave me alone.

Mis hijos tienen hambre, señor.
Pitit mwen yo grangou, Msye.
Y yo también.
Sólo unos centavos, por favor.

Okay. Okay.
Take these twenty cents.
And now, leave me alone.

Gracias, señor.
Me'si, Msye.
Thank you, sir.

CANDOMBLÉ

Bailan.
Saltan los mortales,
Mientras Exú entra triunfalmente,
Y marca con paso inseguro
Los caminos de sus inmensos dominios,
Entre el ritmo de tambores.

Se entrelazan todos,
Confundidos entre un huracán de vientos,
Que desprenden las hojas de los árboles.

Giran.
Giran con atormentado ritmo,
Bañados por la luz de los rayos,
Regalo de Xangó,
Que ha venido a la fiesta
Cabalgando un arcoiris rojo y blanco.

Yansá, se produce entre el aire y la hojarasca y
Deshace al viento
Su largo y negro cabello,
Bañado, ahora, por la luna.

Se mezclan mortales y Orishas.
Exú gira sobre sí mismo,
Recogiendo peticiones de los otros.

Ogún hace su presencia conocida
Por un ensordecedor sonido de metales.

Giran. Giran
Cantan. Cantan

Oxún reparte pétalos
Impregnados en miel libidinosa.

Bailan. Bailan.

Las respiraciones se hacen densas
En el éxtasis del momento.
Los cánticos se elevan al cielo.

BAPTISM

The ocean is shedding light
And the dark-skin men,
One by one,
Enter the immensity of the waters,
Forming a line through all the corners of the universe.

Everyone sings.
Pigeons extend their wings over the bright waters.
Pigeons and men
Confound themselves in a mutual never-felt communion.

I

A strong light covers the men praying in the ocean.
It all happens, *The Mystery*,
In the smallest fraction of time.

Pigeons, Men, the Ocean
Have become One, the Universe, in this Baptismal moment.
One instant. One breath. One time.

There are people observing from the distance.

II

A frail boat is sinking.
A mother embraces her child and offers, in deep, silent communion,
Her only possession
While the others supplicate for the possibility of a new day.
The ocean is shedding light.
Everyone cries.

Pigeons extend their wings over the bright waters.
Pigeons and men
Confound themselves in mutual, never-felt communion.

A strong light covers the refugees praying in the ocean.
It all happens, *The Mystery*,
In the smallest fraction of time.

Pigeons, Men, Ocean
Have become One, *The Universe*,
One instant. One breath. One time.

No one is there to observe.

III

The pigeons fly,
Becoming part of this unique moment.
The Ocean is quiet and peaceful.
Silence
One instant. One breath. One time.
Life's mystery. Death's mystery.
All at once.
Unending.

AND I SAW HIS FIGURE

I saw his figure, transparent, carrying images of incomplete dreams,
And lives made of sand from an immemorial past.
This is how I saw him last night.

But I have seen him, this man, who seems to be my father now,
Rounds of nights, again and again, forever.

And I just can't remember much today of what we spoke
Or in what dreams we have met before.
Perhaps last night, we found each other in the perfect and the subtlest,
Where nothing escapes the knowing, the subconscious recognition.
Not a gesture, not a thought, not a desire.

We conversed last night while the world had its comforting dreaming.
We conversed in that place
Where nothing escapes the transcendental powers of the Soul.

Beyond my daily dreams.
We met last night, once more.

THE SONG OF MY SOUL

The song of my soul.
Glorifies the silence of my deepest world.
Only in this melody, my heart is able to speak with my mind, and
I feel and I dance to the softest and dearest tune.

No words. No books I need.

Myself entering Self in the deepest darkness.
Self, entering myself, quietly.
No need for letting my body go.
No need to suffer, either.

Eternity is here. It will be here, always within my reach.
Just a step deeper every time.
Just a step higher every time.
In the darkest second,
Past the warmest waters.

RAZONES

Debí haber escrito un poema en esta noche.
Me pediste que hablara sobre tí y sobre mí.
Pero no puedo encontrar un sitio tibio aquí en mi alma.
Ayer, sin embargo, todo hubiera sido diferente.

El mar, oscuro y sereno,
Lava con sus frías manos mis descalzos pies en esta noche.
Este frío se me entra por los huesos,
Hasta llegar al alma.

A lo lejos, entre el bullicio y la alegría de la gente,
Escucho el doloroso rasgar de una guitarra.

Entre sollozos, de frente a este mar indiferente, en esta noche clamo.
Y no sé por quien hoy clamo.
Quizás clamo por mí misma.

Siento, que camino por cerrados espacios de nostalgia
Y de sueños recientes, que amenazan escapar.
Siento ser una niña que ha perdido en algún sitio su muñeca.

Y quizás hoy siento más.
Quizás siento temor.
Quizás siento que soy como aquel antiguo amor,
Que se me fué de entre las manos, como se van todas las cosas.
Como se fueron, en un día claro, de mi casa todos mis juguetes.

Este pícaro mar ahora me invita. Y la noche también me invita.
Y yo por primera vez, me siento una con ellos.

Y quisiera, en esta noche sin luna. En esta hermosa noche sin luna.
Poder vestirme con los peces y las algas,
Y cubrir mi cabeza con corales.

Quisiera poder vestirme, en esta noche amiga,
Con la fuerza interna de mi vida.

MOMENTUM

Silence, a song arriving from some distant past,
And the fragrance of the petals fills the air.
Love is singing with majestic voice.
Love. Love. Love—in its highest, most reachable human cognition.

My mind is elated. I can't tell it now from my soul.
Joy, without space, without time.
Only myself and this profound feeling—and you.

I can touch you now
Among the petals scattered by the soft breeze,
And heaven has become my heart.

Singing, Oh, immortal beauty!
Company always present!
I am here, at the center of love!

Silence, myself, and this profound feeling—and my tears,
Searching for the continuity
Of this moment, which is now escaping me.

MACKANDAL

Soft breeze.
He stands in his own silence.
He stands in his own dream.
He stands in his own nature.

He is being watched.
He is being followed.

The rivers to freedom are his path.
A butterfly, a dog,
A singing bird in the bright afternoon
Is his soul.

He speaks.
He suffers.
He struggles.

He knows better, and
His voice is thunder.
He is fire.
He is poison.
He is an angel full of light.

He has transcended time,
For he has come from the past and
He is the future.

He has transcended space,
For he has already done it
In another mountain,
And his space is universal.

Mackandal is God!
For he transmutes.
For he is love
And he is hate.
For he is war
And he is peace.
For he is torture
And he is peaceful dream.

Mackandal!
African warrior.
Soul of mankind!

DEAR OLD NEW FRIEND

You walked away, dear old comrade,
Lost into your own desires for grandeur,
And never again, your eyes looked upon the road
On which we used to dream.

I have, on my own, felt the soft breeze from the other side of the city,
Bringing me now the scent of the unlearned souls,
Those not concerned with texture
But with bread itself to taste,
To satiate existence's hunger.

They care not of what I offer,
but that I offer.

I extend my hands toward them, for you have, somehow, become All.
And they dance and laugh with me
While we all share the simple, daily bread of Life.

I finally rest in happiness, dear old new friend.
Looking at my soul dancing,
Free and safe from vanity.

Joann Rita Vega

BEHIND THESE WALLS

We are all homeless except for the few who have left the cities.
A homelessness whose horrors we cannot fathom.
And there is no home to go to anymore.
We have changed home. We have left home.
We have parched it and closed it with colorless stucco, and we cannot enter it anymore.

We live like outsiders, sometimes peering through half-open windows,
Wondering what lies behind these walls we have built.
Searching for a light inside the room so that we can find a familiar shadow,
A shadow we used to possess but have not seen in the longest time.

We have no home to look into. We remain outside, searching for our own shadows.

Long ago, this used to be called Neuroses,
(Meaning there is a path, a sense of being, lost for a while, but a path to recover),
But today, we have lost our ways, and we do not know it.
We are confused and cannot recuperate from neuroses.

Poor in spirit. Rich in gifts (materials).

The unending run toward possessions. The fear of not possessing something, enough,
Not to share with our brother but to keep and invest while he lies on the street, naked, hungry.
The fear of being. Of simply being.
The fear of thinking. The fear of silence. The fear of meditation.

EL TOCADOR DE CALIPSO

Jonás llegó hoy a la playa,
Como siempre, temprano.
Con su mujer y su hija de ojos grandes
Y piel más clara que la suya.

Cuando el sol salió,
Ya su mujer preparaba
El puesto de frituras
Cerca de la orilla.

Frituras de tiburón muy baratas,
Para que los turistas compren,

Joann Rita Vega

Sentados a la rústica mesa,
Bajo las matas de coco.

La pequeña guitarra de Jonás
Está lista para el improvisado Calipso.

Hoy, como todos los días,
Su música no hablará de él
Ni de sus sueños,
Ni de su lucha por una vida mejor.

Hoy, cantará al turista,
Que lo encuentra todo interesante y bonito,
Hasta el rostro hambriento de Jonás.

Algunas monedas
Le echan en el viejo sombrero,
Mientras Jonás los mira, sonríe, canta y odia.

Cuando el sol ya se pierde
Detrás de las montañas.
Tres figuras con caminar cansado,
Se alejan por la playa.

Jonás, con su guitarra bajo el brazo,
Va contando las ganancias de todo un día
De esconderse a sí mismo detrás de su sonrisa.

¡Maldito!
Dice finalmente, ya en su soledad.
Y su rostro se frunce,
Mientras los tres se pierden por la playa.

GATHERING

Mortals dance!
Drawing a circle of light
While Exu triumphally enters,
Marking with boyish steps
The roads of his vast domains
Among the rhythms of the drums.

They intertwine,
Confounded among a whirlwind
That loosens the leaves of the trees.

They turn.
They spin with tormenting rhythms,
Bathed by the lightning thunders,
A gift from Xango,
Who has come to this celebration
Riding on a red and white rainbow.

Yansa materializes among the air and the foliage,
Undoing her long and bluish hair,
Showered now by moonlight.

Mortals and Orishas mingle,
And Exu turns over himself,
Taking petitions from the others.

Ougun makes his presence known
By a deafening sound of metals.

Dancing.
Dancing.

Singing.
Singing.

Oxun offers rose petals
Impregnated with libidinous honey.
They dance.
They dance.

Breathing becomes dense
In the ecstasy of the moment.
Songs rise to heaven.
Both worlds embrace.

MY SOUL. MY SELF.

The ancient dreams and passages of my mind,
I bring to you.
To this door, which has for an instance opened,
I bring the sorrow and happiness of distant farewells,
Often confounded with encounters.

Opposing wings of the bird of loneliness

I bring, Oh, my Soul,
An old bridge and
A wilted yellow rose.

Joann Rita Vega

The bridge has fallen,
But the rose has not been touched.
And I am here, trespassing this forbidden door.
Advancing through this intimate and unknown trail
That is Myself.

SERENITY

For Ivan.

When I remember
My eyes trying to glimpse beyond these waters
That carry overly intricate secrets
For my human understanding.

Joann Rita Vega

Memories, dreams of past walks,
Picking snails on the shore,
Hand in my father's hand,
Come to meet and hit my heart
With increasing strength,
Vibrating through
All my days, past and present.

My mind rests, unperturbed, still, solemn.
No thought. No reason. No hope.
Only a dream that breaks
For what I am today

And I wonder from the depth of my memories:
Why am I still sensitive to this idea
despite all these long years,
Like the first day I left the shore?

My heart cries.
My soul is lost.
My body is marked with the pain
That belongs to all.
Isolated, as if not understanding,
My mind rests, imperturbable, quiet.
In egocentric serenity,
Away from my heart,
Which now comes to understand me.

SURRENDER

Stars are saluting
With unrecognized knowledge
The deep waters of the ocean.

Surrender.
Surrender.
Surrender.

What do they know
That I am unable to see?

Internal dialogue.
Awakening of consciousness.
Allowing.

Words from the infinite
Composed that absurd call that,
Lost in the light of their non-existent presence,
Echoed a distant thunder.

Transition.
Come to the Cave of Heart.
Surrender.

Printed in the United States
by Baker & Taylor Publisher Services